Value Selling
Business Solutions

For Everyone from
Project Managers to Sales

Bob Turek

1   *Value Selling Business Solutions*

ISBN: 978-0-557-05045-1

To Charlie Baker, a superb salesman, who I learned how to value sell with and who gave me my first value selling consulting opportunity. You are and will be missed.

3   *Value Selling Business Solutions*

Seest thou a man diligent in his business [skilled in his work]? He shall stand before kings; he shall not stand before mean [obscure] men.

-Old Testament, Proverbs 22:29

Contents

- Creating the PSV: Problem Tips
- Creating the PSV: Solution Tips
- Creating the PSV: Value Tips
- A PSV Presentation Exercise

- Introduction to the Case Study: CSM 101-
  Large, Medium Complexity Solution
- Initial Problem Determination Meetings
- PSV Development Meetings
- Redo Your Original PSV Statement

- Elements of a Training, Mentoring,
  Coaching Program (TMCP)
- So, What Did You Learn from This Book?
- The Value of a Value Selling Workshop

- Opportunity for Feedback

9   *Value Selling Business Solutions*

Preface

My introduction to value selling occurred at Aspect Development, an enterprise software solution company in Northern California. In my role as a pre-sales business consultant I was paired up with Charlie Baker, an excellent enterprise software salesman who was also new to the value selling approach. We were both initially skeptical about value selling—we couldn't understand the lack of focus on the solution in the sales training since we both had essentially been solution sellers, versus value sellers, in our software careers.

What surprised me most about Aspect's approach to value selling was that the CEO was part and parcel of it and he convincingly spoke about it. We had never seen a CEO so involved in establishing a sales process that everyone was required to perform. This alone was impressive enough to cause me to dive into the approach—besides we had no choice. We successfully value sold on a couple of deals as we became an excellent sales team. Much of what I have written in this book is based on those experiences.

After Charlie left Aspect he asked me to help him out with establishing value selling at his new company. Value selling in an organization that fully supports it from the CEO on down is one thing—but this new company was new to value selling. Charlie knew that he needed help to get the organization on board. He convinced his boss and the VP of Sales to consider it. We analyzed basic sales processes and presentations to give them the value orientation needed to sell to top level executives. We had to determine whether or not his new company and software solution fit into the value selling model.

That project caused me to reconsider everything I knew about value selling and, in the process, to construct a value selling workshop that conveyed the essential points of it. The workshop focuses on the crucial initial stages of the value sell—the opening, versus closing, processes. Early engagement with top executives, with a clear and powerful process, successfully kicks off these types of deals; the PSV or problem-solution-value approach is therefore the heart of the workshop and this book.

Bob Turek

Agua Dulce, California

Rturek23@aol.com

Value Selling Business Solutions

Chapter 1

Introduction

Value selling is hard. Seasoned sales and pre-sales people complain about the high level of preparation, the need to start at the C-level, early intrusion of an executive sponsor, and holding back on selling the detail software solution until the problem is completely understood. One salesman gave up, reverting to solution-based selling to lower levels in the prospect; he failed miserably in a company committed to value selling.

Value selling on its face is simple; but in practice it is a hard change to make. You have to give up the habit of starting at, and initially gaining significant traction with, any level below a true value based buyer—which is usually at or near the C-level.

How this Book is Organized and Why

Given this track record I've found it is much better to ease people into value selling—slowly revealing the basics followed by advanced concepts that build upon the foundation—so that it opens up like a rose blooms. Consider this chapter the rosebud.

This introduction is followed by an overview of the entire value selling cycle (Chapter 2) and then some sales 101 tips related to value selling (Chapter 3). You will get valuable information about the problem-solution-value approach (Chapter 4) and apply this to a great case study (Chapter 5). Finally, I explain why your attempt to value sell will be much easier if your organization commits to the process (Chapter 6).

The book talks about mastery of seemingly simple concepts that can drastically affect how you approach and perform the value sell. It also includes a great sports analogy to big wave surfing. Analogies solidify understanding. This one is particularly apt because it is so hard to do and requires you to prepare as if your life depended on it.

The Type and Area of Value Selling We Are Dealing With

This book is designed for sales, pre-sales, marketing, technical and executive personnel who are part of the value selling process. The book relates my experience value selling $5-10 million enterprise software solutions while working for Aspect Development as a Business Consultant. Aspect provided what was then called Component and Supplier Management (CSM). CSM is a perfect solution for a value sell because it solved a big problem for manufacturing companies—multiple, out of control design and sourcing entities.

First, I put together a value selling workshop based on my experiences; then I wrote this book based on the workshop. In them, both sales and pre-sales personnel learn how to team up and sell to value focused C-level executives. There is nothing like the actual workshop experience of constructing and presenting value based presentations. However, the book enables me to introduce these concepts to more people and ultimately make the workshops and consulting more effective.

Because the opening, or beginning, of the value sell is so important, we'll focus on these first few meetings with the top executive and his or her direct reports. These meetings are where the value sell is won or lost. Value selling is a team sell including sales, pre-sales, solutions marketing, and executive sponsors. It is highly strategic and demands high levels of preparation. In all of my 20 plus years of managing and performing pre-sales and business consulting roles I never had as much fun and worked as hard as I did in the pressure cooker of C-level value selling.

If you are ready to begin your deals with CEOs, VPs of Operations, General Managers, and other high level value-focused executives, fasten your seat belt and let me relate how we got started in those deals. If you have never done it, I guarantee you will want to try it. You'll be in position to hear a value sold C-level executive say "why haven't we done this already" to which you'll respond "we'll price it according to your value".

My Background

My background should help you understand my viewpoint on value selling. I have 20 years of experience in the enterprise software and consulting business. My experience includes pre-sales, creation and management of pre-sales groups, consulting practice building, sales of consulting services, and project management of ERP, Supply Chain Management (SCM) and Supplier Relationship Management (SRM) solutions. I've been involved in sales of solutions from $200K to $10 million. I've consulted with organizations on value selling, business planning and angel funding. This includes ERP, SCM, leadership training and marketing consulting companies.

Value Selling is a Company-Wide Process

My interest in value selling began upon discovering how my software company could sell large software solutions higher in the organization, for 5-10 times more, qualify deals much sooner, and cut down sales cycle time. This revelation was both inspiring and daunting, yet verified everything I knew about selling large software systems. The company was committed to the process—they required that their solutions be value sold. Value selling can require the entire organization to change to focus on this type of selling—from the CEO to the contract administrator. Everyone who has a role in the process must understand it to support what can be a drastic change in selling processes.

Value selling requires a sales team that includes a business consultant and a solution or technical consultant supporting the head sales person. These aren't necessarily different people—it is more useful to understand that there are different functions that need to be performed. At different times in the sales process different people on the sales team play leadership roles. Once again the emphasis is on the first few meetings with the prospects top executive team—i.e., the opening of the sale.

One of the things you may discover is that you may not want to embark on a value selling process. It takes a certain type of solution, management, and sales team to value sell. In other words, whether or not, and how, it is done varies depending on what is sold, who is selling and who is supporting the sale. You may not have a product that can be sold for 5-10 times what you are now selling it for. You may not have sales people who can successfully present themselves to a top executive team. You may not have the company-wide commitment. Even so, elements of the value sell can be applied to selling anything including projects, proposals, and promotions.

Engagement Versus Access: The Role of the PSV

Engagement, not access, is the focus. In order to engage with top executives the sales team must be doing something that the top executives care about and are interested in. The process is very important, but so is the content of what you are presenting. You have to be ready to be shoved out the door in five minutes, but also be prepared to stay for an hour or two. The level of preparation for these meetings is far beyond what most sales teams have experienced.

Top executive meetings can be chaotic and seemingly unfruitful unless you are prepared for certain "take aways" based on how far the top executive is willing to go with you—with value selling, that can be a long way in a relatively short time. What is needed is a structured approach that is flexible enough to operate in the potentially different time frames and degrees of depth driven by the top executives. That structure is the problem-solution-value (PSV) approach

The PSV approach is fully covered later including an example from a CSM sale, a medium-complexity, enterprise software solution sales process. The example is useful in that it is an excellent representation of a solution that can take full advantage of the value selling process. That value selling process can be easily contrasted with what you sell today and how you sell it.

"If Only I Could….": Introduction to Problem Determination, the First Step in the PSV Approach

Understanding the problem, from the top executive viewpoint, is the first step in value selling. One way to learn about problem determination is to understand the sales team's business problem—i.e., your problem. The problem of value selling can be fleshed out by identifying what are called the salesmen's "if only I coulds":

- If only I could get access to Mr. Big—and once I get access if only I could impress him or her.

- If only I could cut my sales cycle in half and do more deals.

- If only I could sell each deal for 10 times as much.

- If only I could have the best resources whether they be pre-sales, technical, implementation, executive sponsors, etc.

There are many more "if only I coulds" and I invite you to write some down. You've just identified your "problem" related to the "solution" of value selling. This problem identification process is what you must do in relation to your prospect's business. Part of value selling is identifying the prospect's problem and entire PSV. Your goal is to develop a PSV that is powerful and clear that interweaves the problem, solution and value in a way that the prospect's top executive team has never seen before.

It should cause them to say "why haven't we done this already?" There will be a lot more work to do once you get this kind of great reaction. But this is the goal that should be sought in the first few meetings with the top executive and his or her direct reports. It's a tough goal but one that must be reached in order to continue a value selling process. If you stub your toes here you may get a chance to limp back into the top executive's office—but don't count on it.

Effective identification of the problem at a high level of the organization drastically reduces problem definition at lower levels of the organization. It also impresses the top executive because you are revealing a competent and valuable understanding of the business. Knowing the problem helps to more clearly define the solution and the degree to which you need to define it at this point. I can't overstate this—don't go too far with the solution too soon. The focus of your prospect's top executives should be the value of the solution. This is definitely not the case if you enter at the lower levels where the tendency is to focus on the solution and implementation resources.

Basic Value Selling Prospect Types

There are many ways to separate prospect types. One of the most effective differentiations in prospect types in value selling is between the value-based buyer and the "seymours". Seymours want to see more and more and more of the solution—most care little about the problem, let alone the value. You will have to deal with these people at some point— but wouldn't you rather have a top executive who is sold on value first? You may have to prove out the solution to seymours but you will have the power and focus of having sold the value, laced with a full appreciation of the problem and the right solution, from the executive viewpoint. Value selling enables a better understanding in the prospect organization of the PSV and what is really important related to their buying of a product or solution. It focuses the entire prospect organization on what is important to you and them.

This Book is Not....

If you don't know by now this book is definitely not a book about getting access to Mr. Big. There are plenty of materials and training on access. One of the best is Anthony Parinello's book, *Selling to VITO (Very Important Top Officer): Increase Your Commissions by Getting Appointments with Top Decision Makers Today!* This book has proven ways to get access to the top executive that work. But, as we've said before, access is not engagement.

This book is also not:

- How to make a great presentation
- How to sell
- How to manage your manager and your manager's manager
- How to tie revenue to performance metrics
- How to do a detail value assessment project (although we will touch on this important aspect of value selling)

This Book Is....

What is offered is a reasonable approach for a sales team to interact with and to begin the value sell with the top executive and his or her direct reports. It provides a structured way of preparing for and determining the problem, solution and value, linked to implementation phases, at the outset of the value sales cycle. It focuses on the opening of the sale, versus the closing of the sale, through discussions about preparation, interviewing, consolidation of information, presentation, incorporation of feedback and presenting again.

At this point one may say "but I can sell anything if I get access to Mr. Big". Usually a salesman who says this doesn't understand the difference between access and engagement. If you can get access can you sell $10 million solutions? Can you keep Mr. Big's attention? Can you get Mr. Big to invite you back? In other words, are you able to make yourself valuable in Mr. Big's eyes?

Value selling to Mr. Big requires excellent positioning of your company CEO or VP into a deal earlier than you have ever experienced. This necessary evil forces you to qualify whether or not you should be in a deal much sooner. The good news is that you stop working a bad deal. The real good news, if you decide to continue a good deal, is that you embark on a great, high revenue value sell.

Chapter 2

Overview of Value Selling

In order for us to focus on the opening segment of the value sell an understanding of the entire cycle is required. Value selling is an exercise that typically:

- Pushes (versus pulls)
- Educates
- Establishes budgets (versus fitting into existing budgets)
- Occupies evaluation time (takes time away from the competition)

Pushes

In my experience value selling relatively new concepts to manufacturers, especially very high value ones, requires the push-educational approach. A pull-only sell is where the PSV is clear prior to the sales cycle. There is a point in the value sell where you will feel the pull of the prospect—this is the point where they have accepted the value as their own and don't worry too much about what they have to pay for it. For most of the value sell you are pushing.

Educates

The education part of value selling is twofold: 1. Education on your product or solution and the PSV for it, and 2. Education on the value selling process. Prospects aren't used to being value sold. They have to learn how to value buy. If you start with a value-based person or persons this won't be much of a problem. They will be pleasantly surprised by your value selling approach—they'll actually like it. A value-based approach used on a seymour is almost guaranteed to get a bad response. If the prospect is having trouble with your value orientation you may be selling to the wrong person. Even top executives can be seymours. You have to find the value people.

Establishes Budgets

Most value selling does establish and reestablish budgets. The prospect doesn't know how valuable your solutions are. In most organizations no one can approve the larger deals except upper management. Why start at the lower levels just to get hammered at the end by a top executive? Why not start at the top and see if there is potential in the organization to establish the value and pay for a high-value solution. This is where one great result of value selling kicks in—you can qualify out of bad deals sooner.

Occupies Evaluation Time

Value selling allows you to get so firmly entrenched in the prospect's organization that they will not have time to deal with the competition. The only danger here is that your work might be used to justify someone elses products or solution. Done correctly, as the push becomes a pull, you become a partner with the prospect eliminating everyone else far earlier than previously done.

The Steps in the Value Selling Cycle

Here are some of the key steps in a value selling process followed by a few comments about them:

Interest creation
- Company "value" conferences and references
- Initial meetings with C-levels

C-level interaction with sales and pre-sales business consultant
- Initial PSV creation and buyoff
- Sell value assessment

Executive sponsor introduced
- Linked to beginning of detail value assessment

Value assessment
- Interviews, detail value building- *size of this varies depending on access, influence, solution, etc.* Can include solution architecture, project plan and SOW for implementation

- Empowers C-level direct reports and key decision makers/process owners to say "YES" when asked

if these changes can be done and will produce
hard dollar value

- Minimize demonstrations and avoid prototyping

Value Conferences and Same-Industry References

Your company's ability to do conferences that are focused on
value can be extremely helpful. Value conferences can initiate
a sell of something that has a very high value with a very little
definition of the solution. An example of this is where a VP of a
high technology company learned about and internalized the
hard dollar value that a client spoke about at the value
conference. He immediately wanted to engage with us to figure
out how to do it.

This tendency towards action on the part of the top executive,
who is a value-based person, is in stark contrast to the typical
prospect you have probably been dealing with. Understanding
this bias towards action based on value is the key to
understanding why a value sell works with some and not with
others.

We kicked off many of our deals with references in the same
industry as the prospect. In one case the first contact was a

phone call with a VP Operations of a semiconductor equipment company. We briefly discussed his problem, which we were familiar with because a same-industry client had similar issues, followed by an estimate of his potential solution value, which was between $50 and 100 million per year. After he stopped laughing at us we suggested a conference call with the referenced client. He agreed. We did the call, got the VP Operations extremely interested, and started the deal.

Value Assessments

Value assessments are basically small consulting projects designed to fully flesh out the PSV. Value assessments can become deal breakers if done like a classical consulting project that is focused on billable days. It is a *sales* consulting project that in many cases is paid for. It must be very focused and relatively quick as compared to typical consulting projects. The ones I have experience with went from two to nine months in duration—it all depends on the solution, prospect, and your company.

The key here is to make sure that the top executive drives who you deal with on the project and that you guide that choice. You want decision-makers who have the ear of the top executive, who understand the relevant business processes, and who have the capability to identify the relevant budgets and their linkage to the value to your solution. Value assessments are difficult because of the risk of turning it into a typical time consuming consulting project. As we said before this book will not attempt to cover the details of a value assessment process.

The key reason to discuss the entire value selling cycle now is to again emphasize that only a portion of this cycle is dealt with in this book. That area is the initial "C-level (or top executive) interaction..." which includes the problem-solution-value buyoff and potential selling of a value assessment. The most important C-level meetings will occur early in the deal in a value sell—this is completely different from most deals. The PSV structure, so important to have in those initial meetings, will end up being used throughout the value selling process. It becomes the key presentation vehicle for the sales team as it is developed and changed throughout the sales cycle.

Chapter 3

Sales Basics as They Relate to Value Selling

Before we get into the meat of the value sell let's go over some sales basics. As I have said this is not a book on how to sell but there are some basic selling points that are particularly important in value selling. They are:

- Opening a sale (versus closing)
- Role relationships to establish prior to selling
- Listening like you've never listened before
- Preparing like you've never prepared before
- Having the right motives

Opening a Sale

One of the best pieces of sales advice that I have read is the following from a Max Sachs International on-line newsletter:

> We've heard many sales people say the most difficult part of their job is closing the sale. Sometimes the reason may be because the sale was never opened in the first place.
>
> Making a sale involves empathy, rapport and trust between the prospect and the salesperson. The salesperson has to take time to establish rapport...to help the prospect decide that the salesperson has integrity and competence [value]. The salesperson also has to look at the situation through the prospect's eyes [their business issues] to have the empathy necessary to open the sale.
>
> After effectively opening the sale, closing the sale should be the logical conclusion to a well-given presentation.

Opening is even more important in a value sell because of the level of executive you are dealing with and how much value and cost is on the line. Failure in the first few meetings with the top executives could mean never selling to that prospect again.

Role Relationships

The sales process cannot be started until you have established the desired role relationships. You and some members of your team must be perceived as valuable in and of yourselves. The key is you—not your company or product. Your sales team, company and product will naturally follow but must also be value sold. If you start the sales process, which usually has to do with starting to sell the solution, prior to establishing the role relationships you risk losing or, worse yet, being used a column fodder on an RFP or a company-wide educator. Problem determination at the beginning of a deal is a great way to establish the role relationships that position you to perform the value sell.

Listening

Shutting up and listening, after gaining the interest of the top executive with a great reference and asking some open-ended questions, is tough. I've found that the people on the sales team that have the greatest problem with this are the pre-sales consultants. They love to talk about their solution—which is great at the lower levels of the organization because that is what those people want. At the top executive value level, the solution is downplayed. Problem determination is the first engaging exercise with a top executive and requires listening after asking good questions and carefully following up with better questions. Here are some great quotes designed to make you think about how important listening is and how you might be perceived by an executive if you are a bad listener. You don't want a C-level executive reminded of these quotations after dealing with you:

> And 'tis remakable that they
> Talk most who have the least to say.
> > -Matthew Prior, Alma, II

> He that answereth a matter before he heareth it,
> it is folly and shame unto him.
> > -Old Testament, Proverbs 18:13

> They never taste who always drink;
> They always talk who never think.
> > -Matthew Prior, On a Passage..In..Scaligeriana

And finally my favorite:

> Blessed is the man who, having nothing to say,
> Abstains from giving us wordy evidence of the fact.
> > -George Eliot, Theophrastus Such

You must be well prepared with questions but simply going down a list will result in not being invited back. You will be perceived as a nuisance in a nice suit. A value guy will kick you out of his office—this may shock those who are used to the good graces of a seymour type. Good listening techniques such as paraphrasing what you heard and then quickly asking good follow up questions in a conversational style are required.

Preparation and Having the Right Motives

You've got to do your homework. There is no excuse for not doing your research on the company, their industry, and your clients, that match the prospect's needs, before stepping into an executive's office. Vin Scully, a hall of fame broadcaster for the Los Angeles Dodgers, was asked what his secret is for being a great play-by-play broadcaster. He simply said "I do my homework". Scully is famous for his anecdotes on players resulting from his exhaustive research on players. He could fill in any time frame with a great story—many listen to games because of him. He is one of the most valuable people ever to work for the Dodgers.

Personality alone won't cut it with a top executive. You may think that you had a great meeting while the executive is saying "nice guy but what a waste of time". You need to examine your heart prior to going into a meeting with value based buyers because they read people much better than most. If you are half-way prepared, or your motives are not right, you risk failure in the pressure of a top executive meeting. Here is some great wisdom related to motives and preparation:

> Out of the abundance of the heart the mouth speaketh.
> -New Testament, Matthew 12:34

> A double minded man is unstable in all his ways.
> -New Testament, James 1:8

> For he that wavereth is like a wave of the sea driven with the wind and tossed.
> -New Testament, James 1:6 and old surfing proverb

Preparation and empathy with the true needs of your prospect are key components of your personal value to a value-based buyer.

Value Selling is Like Big Wave Surfing

Surfing is a great sport. Big wave surfing is only done by a few great surfers on waves that are 20 feet and higher that could seriously hurt or kill a novice. I've been crushed by 6 footers that contain nowhere near the amount of punishing white water that a big wave contains. I like to compare big wave surfing to value selling because both have a higher degree of preparation, tenaciousness, quickness, creativity, and risk when compared to regular selling and surfing. The comparison is also useful to emphasize several aspects of value selling:

Big Wave Surfing	Value Selling

■ Wave
  ■ Large wave may require tow-in and more preparation
■ Equipment
  ■ Wet suit, board, leash
  ■ Jet ski- for tow-in and rescue
  ■ Helicopter to spot and record
■ Environment
  ■ Swell size and direction
  ■ Wind speed and direction
  ■ Tide height, rising or dropping
  ■ Temperature- air and water
  ■ Location
    ■ Rate at which conditions deteriorate
■ Preparation
  ■ Get in shape for paddling/right equip.
  ■ Study environment to determine when and where to go
	■ Deal
	  ■ Requires more resources and better planning of cycle
	■ Resources
	  ■ Pre-sales, surveys, demos
	  ■ Sales manager
	  ■ Executive sponsor at crucial point
	■ Industry and prospect company
	  ■ Size and positioning
	  ■ Key industry/business issues
	  ■ Key initiatives
	  ■ What do they value
	  ■ What do they need
	    ■ Timing- does my solution fit with needs
	■ Preparation
	  ■ Team must be engaged/cycle planned
	  ■ Detailed research of industry and company

Those new to surfing never think that someone would analyze so much about the swell, wind, temperature, tide height and location to determine when and where to surf. I could go on and on about why a 310 degree swell could be smaller at Rincon Point, near Santa Barbara, than it would be at California Street in Ventura. But, if there is a southeast wind, Rincon's coastal range would block it resulting in better surf conditions.

The point is that you need to do the research in order to pick the right time and place to start. Then you have to execute. Extensive preparation, homework, and follow up is required to succeed. Big waves can require a jet ski to tow you to catch the wave at the right spot and attain the right speed. A paddle in technique on a big wave can be disastrous—mainly because you have to wait until the wave is almost breaking to catch it. Sound familiar? Kind of like being too late in a deal without enough resources. Without the right tools you can catch the wave at the wrong time and be dropped hard and buried under tons of water. Sounds like a bad C-level meeting. There are a lot of waves (deals) and surfers (sales teams) out there but only a few can ride the big ones.

Like the degree of preparation involved in big wave surfing, the value selling sales team must be immersed in the industry, the company, and the task at hand. Look at these big wave surfing photos and relate them to what might be happening in your deals.

It looks like this guy paddled into this one—he caught it late. Notice the frantic body language that indicates that he may be airborne and doesn't know when he will hit the water. He is essentially flying and probably wishes he had a way out—he doesn't.

The wind whipping around this surfer makes the water extremely choppy. He probably shouldn't be out there. The guy on the left is thinking "Uh oh, he's gonna eat it!". This makes me think about a C-level prospect that gave bad feedback to an executive sponsor about his salesman.

This surfer brings to mind the smoothest, most experienced salespeople I have worked with. The wave is huge but he is riding it just right and is aware of it's power, direction and behavior. The only problem is that he is all alone; value selling, as compared to big wave surfing, is a team sport. So, we need a team surfing picture.

This picture is from a movie shoot from a recent James Bond film. It's more challenging to surf with a team. They have to give each other room to operate on their section of the wave. One team member cannot move without knowing the effect on his or her team. It requires focused awareness of each other and what they are doing. The cameraman in the helicopter is communicating with the surfers, positioning them and offering a viewpoint that they can't see.

Consider the timing of roles in your deal. The salesperson surfs in front, a business consultant close behind, with a technical resource zooming in at just the right time. The support personnel are riding different parts of the wave performing their different roles in the deal. The executive sponsor from your company, possibly your CEO, is in the helicopter waiting for the opportune time to drop in at your direction.

The wave represents the prospect and the deal. It's being ridden and analyzed by many people in order to achieve the best outcome. The white water is a great representation of tasks already done. If you get caught in it you are probably repeating poorly done tasks and losing control. Reminds me of a bad value assessment with seymours grabbing and knocking you off your value board.

Keep this picture in your mind when you are team value selling. If the sales team is doing it's job, the prospect will love the ride, having never been ridden like this before, and will see things in ways they have never seen.

One final note: You Should Be Selling to Top Executives

If you have any doubts about whether value selling works and whether you should be riding the big waves, consider my inspiration for selling to the top executive:

> Seest thou a man diligent in his business [skilled in his work]? He shall stand before kings; he shall not stand before mean [obscure] men.
> -Old Testament, Proverbs 22:29

It's a lot more fun selling to kings than it is to obscure men. But value selling requires a team that must be coordinated and firing on all cylinders. Diligence, preparation, listening, empathy and developing interest are prerequisites to C-level value selling. Just as an exciting ride ends with a gentle move of your surfboard over the last remnant of the wave, a great deal, properly value sold, ends with a smooth, seamless closing of the deal.

Chapter 4

Value Selling Using the Problem, Solution, Value (PSV) Approach

Value Selling Team Requirements

The value selling sales team can consist of many players especially in large software solution deals. Sales team functions in this type of deal include:

Salesperson- operates at C-level and VP level. Establishes value of self and team at C-level.

Business Consultant (BC)- operates at C-level, VP-level and lower levels. Is the key value consultant with a strategic role from start to finish. Will run the value assessment and most of the problem-solution-value messaging up to and beyond that point.

Solution Consultant (SC)- operates at director and lower levels. Technical role with emphasis on solutions to be deployed. Does demonstration, prototyping, and provides technical expertise.

These functions can overlap. They are not necessarily separate people—especially in the case of business and solution consultants. The BC and SC could be the same person but the roles require very different types of skills. People tend to migrate to one or the other. The BC must be a seasoned person who can hang tough with a top executive. The focus here should be on functions required versus people although in the size deals that I worked on you needed a separate person for each role. At times we needed more people to assist the BC especially during the value assessment project.

One Key Goal of the Initial C-level Interaction: Sell a Value Assessment

As we have said, preparation is paramount. Preparation for the initial meetings includes industry/company research, deep familiarity with same industry references, meeting input from previous meetings, customized questionnaires, and other relevant information. You cannot over-prepare—you can't strategize enough. The salesperson and business consultant will meet with the C-level and possibly direct reports to determine business issues/initiatives, barriers to buying, solution requirements, and value. A lot of this information is preliminary and developed further as you go through the cycle.

Upon being invited back, the return meetings are to present and discuss what was learned in a problem-solution-value (PSV) format and gain initial value buy-off. It may take a few meetings to get to this point. It depends on how good you are at running a value selling process. The goal of this initial set of meetings, the heart of the value sell, should be to gain a buy-off on conducting a value assessment. If the initial executive contact is the heart, then the value assessment can be viewed as the body of the value sales cycle.

The value assessment requires gaining access and engaging with decision makers and business process owners to flesh out a detail solution architecture, business processes, and value. The goal of the value assessment is to enable the decision-makers and process owners to say "yes" when the C-level asks "can you implement the solution and get the value?" We will not cover details about how to conduct a value assessment here. It can be a very complex process requiring all the skills of the sales team.

Preparation for and Performing of the Initial C-level Interview

This initial meeting or set of meetings may be with the C-level and a few direct reports. Question and issue sheets that are standardized by solution and industry must be customized based on research and communications with the prospect. Same-industry reference information must be ready for use at the appropriate time.

The emphasis at this point should be on assessment, not selling the solution. Remember that part of assessing is problem determination and establishing your individual value. Assessing the situation requires establishing the fact that you are interested in the prospect's business and their most important business issues. The same-industry reference material is weaved in to establish the fact that other companies have implemented the solution and gained specific value with it. The client reference material goes a long way in establishing the credibility of your solution in this initial phase of the value sell—in other words, don't oversell the solution. The goal is to get invited back to present a more cohesive problem-solution-value statement. It cannot be overemphasized that value and problem definition is paramount. The worst thing you can do in these initial meetings is to prattle on about the details of the solution— especially when you don't understand the problem.

The Questionnaire

The business consultant customizes the questionnaire used in problem determination. One page is ideal. It should be used to prompt yourself only. Use it to carry on a conversation, constantly summarizing, paraphrasing back the answers obtained from the executives, and to quickly ask logical follow up questions. Remind yourself to listen, listen, listen. This is the business consultant's chance to establish personal value.

The following is an example of a one page questionnaire having to do with a CSM sale. It focuses on a part of CSM called Strategic Sourcing. Use this is to get a feel for the amount of detail you should be taking into the initial meetings:

General
    Numbers of Divs., ERPs, parts, commodity codes, suppliers
    Different schemes for parts, commodity codes, suppliers
    Mergers/acquisitions
    Corporate initiatives to reduce expense/costs

Strategic Sourcing approaches
    Spend coverage/breakdown by commodity- what is limiting coverage?
    How gather spend, inventory, demand- how long is process? Accuracy? Completeness?
    Corporate control/assistance with commodity management
    Organization- commodity management team? Functions?
    How do you id candidate commodities for sourcing improvements?
    Strategic commodity plan? (business case for sourcing decisions through next contract- yields commodity and supplier focus)
    PPV measurement- across division variance?
    Time to negotiate/innovate?

Supplier Management- local vs. global
    How do you know every part of the org. is paying same price for same mat'l/item?
    Strategic vs. other suppliers—how many and how do you choose them?
    How do you know supplier performance is poor? Agree on measures and metrics?
    How qualify suppliers? How long is process? Is it consistent across org.?
    Formal reviews with suppliers- circumstances that cause review/ frequency/preparation and info. gathering/central or local— contracts RFQ processes
    How allocate spend to suppliers- volume purchase agreements vs. allocation
    Plan how many suppliers is optimal, which type, by commodity?
    How phase in or phase out? Measure delivery, quality, obsolescence, contract perf./expiration

Part rationalization/commodity code projects
    Degree of commonality? Duplication? Take advantage of functional equivalents?
    Innovation focus

After gaining information in the initial problem determination meetings, the business consultant has a lot of work to do. Information is obtained that needs to be consolidated, formulated and presented in an expert fashion in a problem-solution-value format. This is where many sales teams break down because they don't understand how much work it takes to put together materials for a working session presentation that truly results in a "why haven't we done this before" reaction. The team should be constantly assessing the presentation given this high standard.

Creating the PSV: Problem Definition Tips

The problem statement must reflect the most important business issues, initiatives and buying barriers. Ultimately the prospect will agree with, and take ownership of, this problem statement. The first time it is presented will be in a rough working copy form so that all parties can work with it and gain agreement.

The problem opens the door to presenting your solution. The issues, initiatives, barriers should be ranked according to their importance and relationship with each other.

Creating the PSV: Solution Definition Tips

The biggest mistake sales teams make is presenting too much solution too soon. At this point the solution should be as generic as possible using the prospects terminology. Don't get bogged down teaching the prospect the names of your specific solutions. Avoid detailed discussions of solutions and rattling off solution features. Good potential value, with a relatively low emphasis on the solution, will be appreciated by the C-level executive. Remember that you have a process for determining the detail solution as it applies to the prospect—the value assessment. At this point the prospect wants to learn that a solution to their business problem is recognized, is available, and could be extremely valuable.

Creating the PSV: Value Definition Tips

Value must be presented in terms that the prospect understands and identifies with. Only value that a prospect is likely to buy-off on should be formally presented. Don't throw all possible value points at the prospect. Presenting all possible value points can seem good because a lot of value can be presented. It is usually bad to do this because it degrades the overall believability of the value. The result in the prospects mind is less perceived value and confusion on what parts of the value are real.

The overall business case must be driven home by linking the value to the solution and the original problem. This linkage of problem, solution, and value is the heart of the presentation. If your presentation seems to present the problem, solution and value as separate elements, i.e., the problem points don't begin to integrate well with the solution points and the value points, then you are not ready. If you don't begin to see the various PSV points firing off in your mind as a related whole, then your prospect won't be seeing something that "they have never seen before" and won't be excited about going ahead.

Differentiate between hard dollars and soft dollars. Hard dollars are associated with bottom line profitability. One example in relation to Strategic Sourcing is spend or cost of purchased parts—not just the cost of purchasing processes but the parts themselves. Every dollar of spend reduction goes to the bottom line profit. Not all hard dollar items are this clear. In a manufacturing environment, spend reduction associated with less vendors and parts to deal with can have tremendous downstream cost reduction also. These downstream costs are softer but can be very large and therefore significant.

Soft dollar value is associated with things like time-to-volume and time-to-market. This is not to say that these items will not drive a prospect to purchase your solution—it is saying that these are harder to clearly identify in terms of real, hard dollars. Productivity is another soft dollar item that by itself does not get people excited. Inventory reduction is "soft" because it is generally seen as a cash flow item. Enabling new business services like bill of material sourcing for the prospect's customers can be very valuable but again may be difficult to quantify clearly.

Use the hard dollars to increase the credibility of the soft dollars. The ideal situation is one where the prospect buys off on hard dollar items and starts telling you how important the soft dollar items are. An attitude of "let's work together to maximize the benefits" is a sure indication that the prospect is buying off on your value sell. Now the pull, versus the push, of value selling should start to rear it's head. Finally, your recognition that there is a difference between hard and soft dollar value tells the top executive that you are interested in making a serious impact on the business.

A PSV Presentation Exercise

A workshop on value selling would proceed just about the same way as this book has. We opened up the concept of value selling in the introduction, followed by an overview of the value selling cycle with emphasis on a specific portion of that cycle, followed by details about the initial C-level interaction, C-level interviews, and putting the problem-solution-value statement together. Now we will begin to apply what we've learned—first with a PSV presentation construction exercise.

One of the useful preparation exercises that I have people do prior to attending a workshop is to try doing a simple PSV statement for one of their current deals. This task accomplishes a few things:

1. It forces you to think in a PSV format
2. It makes you realize that you may not have enough information to do a PSV
3. If makes you realize that possibly all you know is the "S"

Here is a review of the PSV tips that we covered:

Problem

- Statement of business issues and initiatives that are important to the prospect- rank, open door to solution

Solution

- Genericize and use prospects terms
- The prospect wants to learn that a solution to their business problem is recognized and available

Value

- Value that prospect is likely to buy off on
- Do not throw all possible value points at prospect
- Drive home the business case by linking the value to the solution and the original problem
- Your recognition of "hard" vs. "soft" dollars tells executive that you are interested in making an impact on his bottom line

Presentations are structures around which you present your business case. Looking at presentations as structures is very useful—what do your structures convey to your prospect? Are they grand and majestic like a mighty mountain? Can they cause a person to stand in awe as if you were staring up at an imposing skyscraper? Or are they like a shanty in the poorest part of town in a third world country? Take a look at this mountain. It is striking, clear, and settles you down. You start to think big thoughts and get ready for action.

The structure is crucial to convey the importance and gravity of what you are presenting. I'm not talking about pretty colors and graphics. I'm talking about content. One of the best presentations I have ever seen was about 6 slides with 4-5 bullets per slide—and no fancy graphics. The structure, clarity, and confidence with which it was presented helped win a $4 million consulting contract. A shanty structure presented to a high level executive fails; immediately you have to fight the perception that you are poorly prepared without clarity and purpose. This picture of a once popular surfing spot overrun by local hoodlums reveals the confusion and lack of purpose you must avoid with your prospect.

You want your prospect to come to your mountain and stand in awe at it's clarity, power and beauty. Remember, your prospect should be saying "Wow! Why haven't we done this already?"

I'm not here to tell you that you need an agenda and to close with a "next steps" slide. You do need to do these things—but my advice is to concentrate on a simple, powerful, and clear structure with content that gets attention.

Given the tips on problem, solution and value creation, try constructing a PSV statement for one of your current deals. Try to do only 1-2 slides for each area- 1-2 slides for the problem, 1-2 slides for the solution and 1-2 slides for the value. Back up material is fine but 3-6 slides for the main points is crucial. This forces you to focus and makes it a lot easier to integrate the problem, solution and value. After you've done this you will be prepared to better understand the case study in the next chapter.

Chapter 5

A Value Selling Case Study

Introduction to the Case Study:

CSM 101- Large, Medium Complexity Solution

We introduced CSM, Component and Supplier Management, in the first chapter as a software based solution that can be value sold successfully. It deals with Strategic Sourcing and what is called Strategic Design solutions for a manufacturing company.

A one sentence PSV for CSM is:

> CSM solves the problem of multiple divisions with costly different part numbering, design and sourcing approaches by centralizing and cross-referencing of this

information leading to spend reduction through increased ability to negotiate and buy in volume.

A lot is lost in simplifying CSM to this extent. It is done here to allow you to get your arms around the concept. The following is a very high-level problem-solution-value statement for a generic, meaning not yet specific to a prospect, CSM application. This is the type of PSV statement that you should have in your hip pocket for an executive elevator conversation. The problem, solution, and value points will be customized and enhanced for a prospect:

Problem- direct material/components/designs/sourcing uncoordinated

- Multiple part numbering schemes
- Duplication, no comparison information for functional equivalent analysis
- Multiple ERP instances/systems
- Multiple design groups feeding off each other
- Uncoordinated buying
- No spend analysis across divisions
- Downstream costs as a result- design, purchasing, manufacturing, inventory control

Solution- centralized content management enabling strategic sourcing and strategic design

- Enables cross referencing and parametric analysis of design attributes to drastically decrease duplication and enable functional equivalent analysis by design and sourcing
- Strategic sourcing including multi-division spend analysis by vendor and vendor parents down to grade, type, attributes, technology skill
- Strategic design including reuse management and preference management in use of parts on designs

Value- hard vs. soft dollar--may be new type of business
- Hard dollar: 10-15% spend decrease,
- Soft dollar: Time-to-volume/market improvement, design, inventory, purchasing, manufacturing, productivity, etc.
- Valuable services enabled- potential for differentiation and revenue

An important point is that not all of a solution, or set of solutions, may be applicable to a given client at a given time. This may not be because they can't use it—it may be because the value isn't high enough—yet. When using a value sell you have to decide how many of, and when, your solutions should be pushed in a given sales effort. Strategic Sourcing, one of the

CSM solutions, might be sold in one deal followed by Strategic Design in another deal. It could be that Strategic Design could be much more valuable, and easier to sell and implement, with Strategic Sourcing in place. The point to be made here is that the value sell can change the way you sell your stable of solutions and allow you to establish much longer, active, valuable relationships with your clients.

The slides in this chapter include those from a typical value selling sales cycle. They represent a composite view of several sales cycles. They are not all necessarily prospect presentation slides. Some, like the first three problem, solution and value slides, were initially internal to the sales team to help them develop the problem, solution and value. The value is in allowing you see the step-by-step process of problem determination and PSV development.

Initial Problem Determination Meetings

Initially an hour long problem determination meeting was held with a VP of Corporate Supply Chain Management (SCM) and the direct reports of a multi-billion dollar manufacturer of medical equipment—about five people were in attendance in addition to the sales team of three. A questionnaire similar to the example in Chapter 4 was used. The goal of the initial meeting was to gain enough information about the problem to put an excellent, but preliminary, PSV statement together from which a working session could be conducted. The value of the sales team was established in this initial meeting because of the ability to quickly develop rapport through a genuine interest and understanding of the prospects business and industry.

PSV Development Meetings

The next meeting consisted of a PSV working session. It was designed to work through what we learned via a problem-solution-value format. Value of the sales team continued to be enhanced along with the value of the solution in this follow on meeting. The goal of this meeting is to work together with the prospect to cut down, and integrate, the bullet points. One key was to attempt to eliminate the barriers to buying that were identified in the first meeting.

A key slide is the value roadmap slide that matches a potential implementation sequence with the value potential at each step. Again, depending on the client, an attempt at this may be premature. It's real value was to help focus and pare down the PSV statement. Overall value in dollars can be estimated based on a credible client reference at this point. The value in the road map was tied to implementation steps without identifying the dollar value. Value can be specifically filled in as you find it—and definitely proven during the detail value assessment.

The first slide below began the PSV working session which followed the initial information gathering meeting. It outlines the partnering process along with the goal of the specific session.

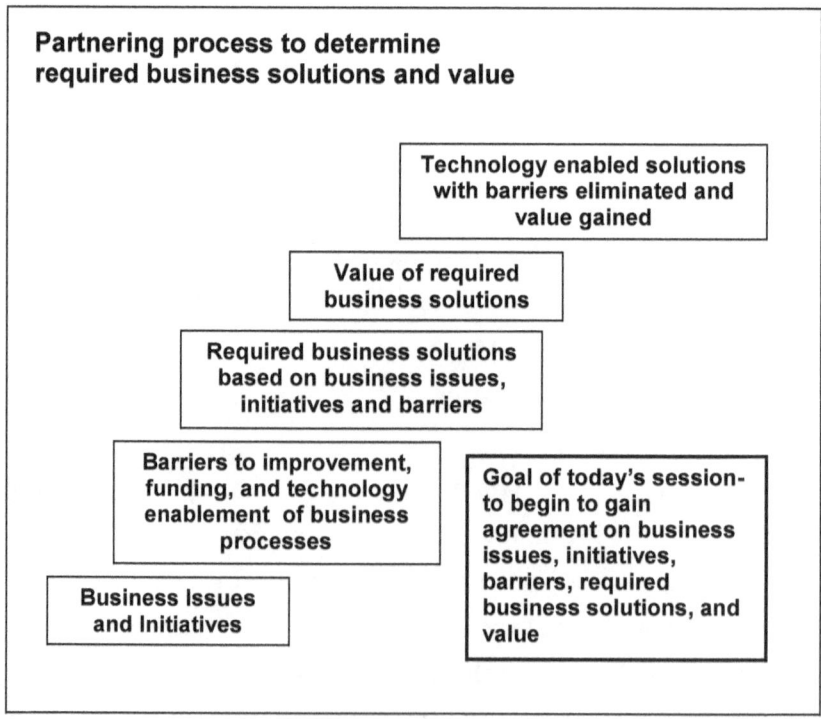

The next four slides are rough working copies of the problem, barriers, solution and value. These slides are the result of many hours of work after the initial information gathering meetings. They are too detailed for a formal PSV presentation designed to sell the value assessment and probably need scrubbing to be used in a working session—but they are close to what could be used. The goal is to reveal that you have been listening well and have an intense interest in understanding their business. Even these rough slides can begin to reveal a picture that the prospect has never seen before.

The attendees for the working session were the VP Corporate SCM, direct reports and a couple of lower level business process experts. You have to determine the level of detail to cover given time constraints, personalities, and guidance from prospect members. If not controlled well—and/or you haven't identified the PSV candidate items well—the working session may not result in a step forward.

Note that in this case the prospect didn't like the term "problem" so we used "business issues". The "barriers" slide was particularly useful in this instance because through the initial PSV process we were able to virtually eliminate them. Barriers are usually not made a focal point of discussions with the prospect this early but we knew that we could counter them early.

Business issues and initiatives

- *Cost of quality* measurement (not done today) and control
    - Alignment with FDA- confidence in hitting production date- degree to which alterations to design, schedule, availability (which affect manufacturing variability) can be controlled to better align with FDA release
    - Missed production date results in high inventory, missed higher initial margins/selling prices/first to market

- *"Use internet to greatest advantage"* - Prospect's annual report:
    - Collect and monitor patient data
    - Transaction support in supply chain management and purchasing
        - note: differentiate this from longer term strategic activities

- *Strategic sourcing*- spend analysis by supplier
    - Want standardized approaches- e.g., strategies per commodity team
    - Commodity management- Division commodity team approach as model

- *Commodity coding scheme standardization*

- *Total cost* analysis

- *SCM and ERP* business solutions implementation

- *Cost reduction that can directly affect funding of innovation*

- *Outsourcing* trend- CRM division- AVL linking

- *Supplier consolidation*

- *Supplier qualification and certification*- modeling after auto/hi tech

- *Phasing in and phasing out suppliers*- demand planning

- *Lean manufacturing*- one division as model
    - Manufacturing has decreased cost but inventory has increased along with product mix increase

- Move toward *Dell business model*- cost of quality and availability limitations

> Rough working copy made after initial meeting

Barriers to improvement, funding, and technology enablement of business processes

- *Innovation focus* and high margins of company makes cost reduction programs harder to justify
    - Hard dollar cost reduction, e.g., spend, not linked to more funding for innovation?
    - Business solution value not linked to cost of quality/manufacturing variability/time to market- need to develop link to both short term and long term supplier management via technology enabled business solutions
- *Focus on "getting business processes and organizations in place first"* prior to "technology"
    - note: a critical mass of business processes cannot be done without technology enablement; e.g.,
        - Timely spend analysis by part/commodity- requires structured content and decision support solution to analyze,
        - Notification/response/reaction to supplier availability/schedule issues- requires technology to enable quick resolution of schedule and availability problems
    - note: organizations can be put together and trained in line with implementation of technology enabled business processes
- *Data/content/information availability* in a repeatable, sustainable business process
    - Current spend analysis only spend by supplier
    - Data gathering task to obtain spend by commodity and part requires too much resource and time
    - D&B project not integrated with structured content required for complete spend analysis
- *Expending budget and resources on costly programs* that may be difficult to complete
    - Commodity code scheme standardization (vs. cross referencing approach)
    - D&B information development related to supplier management with non-structured content approach
- *Focus on short term solutions to business issues*
    - For example: supplier design issue affects supply availability, manufacturing variability and time to market
        - Short term problem solving solution: quicker response with technology enabled business process to communicate schedule/availability
        - Long term problem solving solution: strategic sourcing/commodity/supplier management strategies/programs to help assure supply
- *Cost of quality and availability* need improvement to enable *Dell business model*

> **Rough working copy made after initial meeting**

Required business solutions- based on business issues, initiatives and barriers

- *Structured content* that cross references parts, commodities, suppliers
    - Does not require adoption of standardized commodity coding scheme by all divisions/entities;
    - D&B value integrated- risk management, supplier hierarchies combined to perform more valuable spend aggregation and analysis

- *Technology enabled strategic sourcing*
    - Commodity management through spend analysis by supplier, commodity hierarchy and part
        - Commodity planning, strategic suppliers/commodities yielding more stability in supply base
    - Global supplier management
        - Performance (technology, quality, responsiveness, delivery, cost, collaboration),
        - Allocation of spend- negotiate and execute
        - Stabilization of supplier base in terms of quality, schedule and delivery

- *Supply schedule and capacity collaboration*
    - Short/mid term problem solving- formal technology enabled business process to reveal and respond to deviations quickly (avoid time lag associated with identification of problem, reactions, responses)
    - Mid/long term planning- schedule, capacity
    - Leverage other pre-existing SCM solutions to enable collaboration

- Next steps
    - Design analysis with structured content- duplicates at source manufacturer, functional equivalents analysis, business rules for choosing from alternative parts/suppliers (usage, cost, etc.)
    - Negotiation and contracts managed on a global basis
    - Multi level outsourcing management

> **Rough working copy made after initial meeting**

Value of required business solutions

- *Cost of quality/manufacturing variability decreased* and time to market confidence increased through short and long term supplier management and strategic sourcing

- *Ease of mergers and acquisitions* with different systems and schemes-
    - Quick spend aggregation, incorporation and leverage- even with different part, commodity and supplier coding schemes

- *Enables and provides foundation for negotiation and innovation* internally and with suppliers
    - Supplier innovation- design and sourcing, e.g., inventory management techniques, focus on total cost, next step design collaboration, "Dell model" with suppliers, etc.

- *Spend reduction-* bottom line profit that could be funneled to product innovation

- *Inventory reduction*

- *Productivity improvement*

- *Part introduction and control cost reduction*

- *Reduction or elimination of cost of non-value add programs*

> Can you afford to wait? Key benefit is time-to-value by partnering with our content services, consulting and software solutions.

> Rough working copy made after initial meeting

A summary slide including business issues, barriers, solution and value was used to give all working session attendees a big picture. This big picture view allows the group to connect the dots between the problem, solution and value and begin to see how barriers to proceeding can be eliminated. At this point the working session became a highly productive meeting because the problem, solution, and value began to be integrated. This "marking up" process is crucial to begin the prospect's ownership of the PSV. Another meeting or two with individuals and subgroups may be necessary to present the final view of the PSV that prompts the selling of a value assessment.

Notice that the connect-the-dots slide reveals that most of the business issues have to do with content and strategic sourcing solutions. It became apparent that the scheduling and capacity collaboration solution was simply not addressing key problems. This same solution revelation became apparent when the value points were connected—once again structured content and strategic sourcing created most of the value. The next slide, "marking it up...", italicizes the items that were identified as "keepers". We even agreed on some preliminary value points. At this point the "why haven't we done this already" mentality begins to take hold and a push for a value assessment begins with comments like "let's determine if the value is real".

Preparation: summarize and connect the dots…be able to explain the connections…get buy off on critical items--hard dollars vs. soft dollars

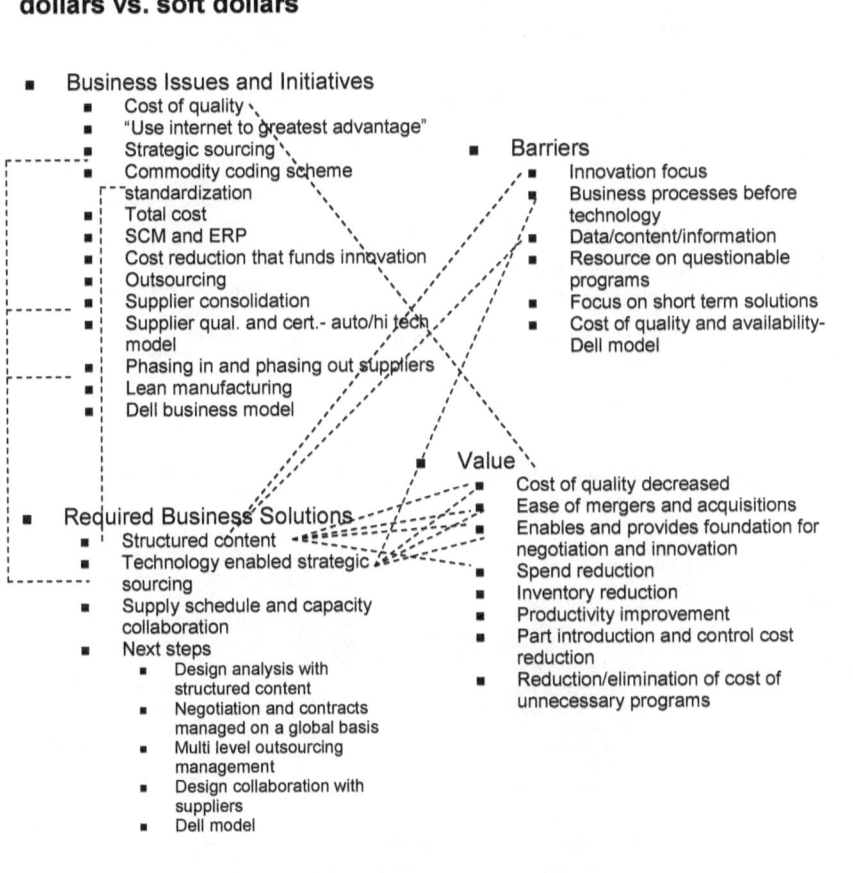

- Business Issues and Initiatives
  - Cost of quality
  - "Use internet to greatest advantage"
  - Strategic sourcing
  - Commodity coding scheme standardization
  - Total cost
  - SCM and ERP
  - Cost reduction that funds innovation
  - Outsourcing
  - Supplier consolidation
  - Supplier qual. and cert.- auto/hi tech model
  - Phasing in and phasing out suppliers
  - Lean manufacturing
  - Dell business model

- Barriers
  - Innovation focus
  - Business processes before technology
  - Data/content/information
  - Resource on questionable programs
  - Focus on short term solutions
  - Cost of quality and availability- Dell model

- Value
  - Cost of quality decreased
  - Ease of mergers and acquisitions
  - Enables and provides foundation for negotiation and innovation
  - Spend reduction
  - Inventory reduction
  - Productivity improvement
  - Part introduction and control cost reduction
  - Reduction/elimination of cost of unnecessary programs

- Required Business Solutions
  - Structured content
  - Technology enabled strategic sourcing
  - Supply schedule and capacity collaboration
  - Next steps
    - Design analysis with structured content
    - Negotiation and contracts managed on a global basis
    - Multi level outsourcing management
    - Design collaboration with suppliers
    - Dell model

Result after prospect working session(s)... if they are marking it up they are "owning" it!

- Business Issues and Initiatives
  - *Cost of quality*
  - "Use internet to greatest advantage"
  - *Strategic sourcing not technology enabled*
  - *Don't need Commodity coding scheme standardization*
  - Total cost
  - SCM and ERP
  - Cost reduction that funds innovation
  - *Outsourcing*
  - *Supplier consolidation*
  - Supplier qual. and cert.- auto/hi tech model
  - Phasing in and phasing out suppliers
  - Lean manufacturing
  - *Dell business model- needs definition in our industry*

- Barriers
  - *Innovation focus- compatible with/helped by solution*
  - *Business processes before technology-strat srcing ex*
  - *Data/content/information-content mgmt. solves*
  - Resource on questionable programs
  - Focus on short term solutions
  - Cost of quality and availability-Dell model

- Required Business Solutions
  - *Structured content*
  - *Technology enabled strategic sourcing*
  - Supply schedule and capacity collaboration
  - *Next steps*
    - *Design analysis with structured content- move up/FE capab.*
    - *Negotiation and contracts managed on a global basis*
    - *Multi level outsourcing management*
    - *Design collaboration with suppliers*
    - Dell model

- Value
  - *Cost of quality decreased- need to id cost factors*
  - Ease of mergers and acquisitions
  - Enables and provides foundation for negotiation and innovation
  - *Spend reduction- 10% of $1B spend = $100M in first year*
  - Inventory reduction
  - Productivity improvement
  - *Part introduction and control cost reduction- co.study of mfg., invent., QA costs 10K/part 3K PIC decrease = $30M first year*
  - Reduction/elimination of cost of unnecessary programs

Why haven't we done this already?
Let's do something to determine if the value is real, i.e., detail value assessment

The next slide, "relatively unimportant points eliminated...",
reveals a simple, clear, and powerful PSV taking shape. This is
a turning point slide. The prospect really appreciates this
process because they are truly seeing things that they have
never seen before. For example, they thought that they had to
re-engineer their strategic sourcing processes before
considering software technology. Rather they discovered that
"we need your technology to enable strategic sourcing"; and
thus a key barrier to buying was eliminated.

Another seemingly insurmountable barrier was the company's
"innovation focus". They didn't want anything to dampen the
innovation of their design resources. But they realized that
needless design proliferation severely impacted the company.
They began to see that our solution would not only help them
control their innovation problem, by easy identification of
similar designs for reuse given the enhanced part technical
content, but it would actually allow them to be more
innovative because design resources would be freed up. The
PSV approach unearths these types of revelations and
therefore goes a long way in terms of establishing your team's
value to the prospect.

Result after prospect working session(s)... relatively unimportant points eliminated; P, S & V begin to clarify

- Business Issues
  and Initiatives
  - Cost of quality
  - Strategic sourcing not
    technology enabled
  - Outsourcing
  - Supplier consolidation

- Barriers (are solved!)
  - Innovation focus-
    compatible with/helped
    by solution
  - Business processes
    before technology-we
    need technology to
    enable strategic sourcing

- Required Business Solutions
  - Structured content
  - Technology enabled
    strategic sourcing

- Value
  - Spend reduction- 10% of
    $1B spend = $100M in first
    year
  - Part introduction and
    control cost reduction-
    co.study of mfg., invent.,
    QA costs 10K/part-3K PIC
    decrease = $30M first year

> *Why haven't we done this already?*
> *Let's do something to determine if the*
> *value is real, i.e., detail value assessment*

The value roadmap should be done with a full understanding
of the prospects tolerance for confusion—i.e., it can be very
powerful or extremely confusing depending on the success
that you've had developing the solution and sequence of value.
At this point they may be able to buy off on the total value but
may have trouble breaking it up according to the
implementation of specific solutions.

A good value roadmap at this stage, before the value
assessment, requires extremely good knowledge of a client
reference that has implemented in the same industry as the
prospect. You may or may not add breakdowns of the time
phased value numbers—here it was enough to understand
generic value with the idea that the detail value would be
proven in the value assessment.

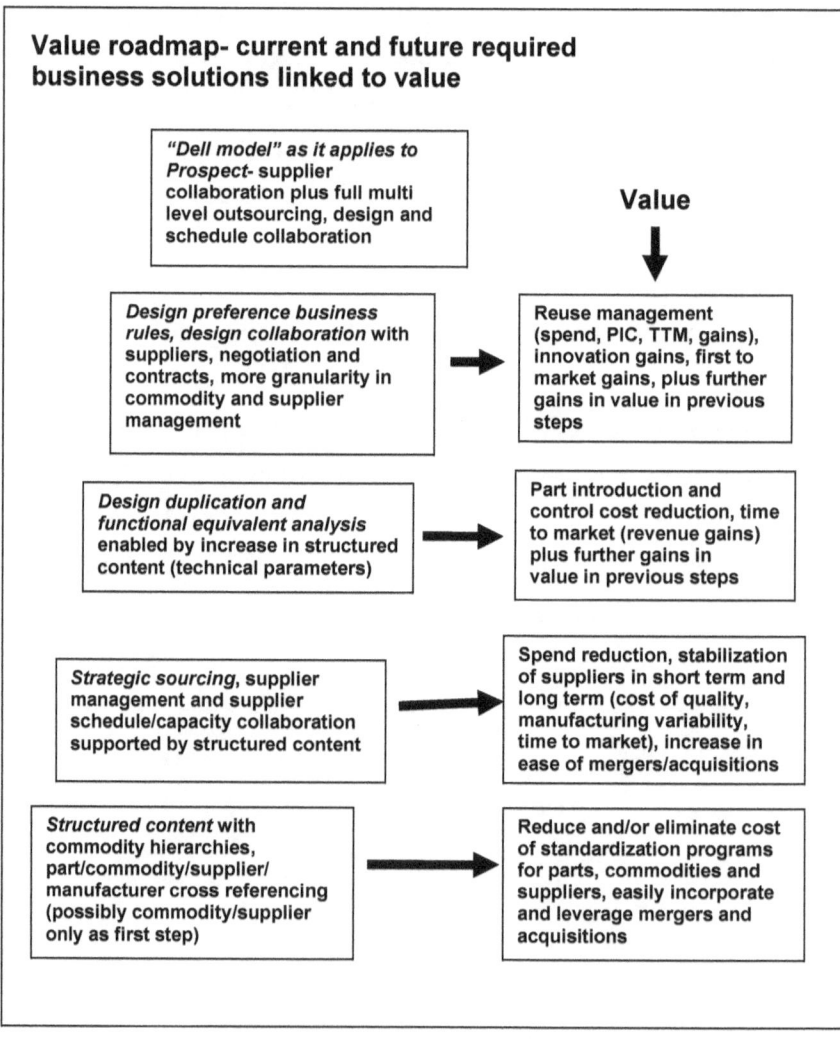

Value roadmap- current and future required business solutions linked to value

"Dell model" as it applies to *Prospect*- supplier collaboration plus full multi level outsourcing, design and schedule collaboration

Value

Design preference business rules, design collaboration with suppliers, negotiation and contracts, more granularity in commodity and supplier management

Reuse management (spend, PIC, TTM, gains), innovation gains, first to market gains, plus further gains in value in previous steps

Design duplication and functional equivalent analysis enabled by increase in structured content (technical parameters)

Part introduction and control cost reduction, time to market (revenue gains) plus further gains in value in previous steps

Strategic sourcing, supplier management and supplier schedule/capacity collaboration supported by structured content

Spend reduction, stabilization of suppliers in short term and long term (cost of quality, manufacturing variability, time to market), increase in ease of mergers/acquisitions

Structured content with commodity hierarchies, part/commodity/supplier/ manufacturer cross referencing (possibly commodity/supplier only as first step)

Reduce and/or eliminate cost of standardization programs for parts, commodities and suppliers, easily incorporate and leverage mergers and acquisitions

This discussion and the slides revealing the build up of the PSV statement reveals that the real value selling happens when the working sessions occur. It is here where the prospect participates in the building of the PSV and the selling of the value assessment begins. Once agreement on the PSV is obtained, selling the value assessment to "prove out" the potential value is a natural next step. Your team has proven it's worth and the prospect should be more than ready to allow you to come in and perform a very high value, quick consulting project that could include a detailed implementation plan and statement of work for the project.

Redo Your Original PSV Statement

Given the case study information you should be armed with many ideas about how to change your original PSV. At this point in a workshop everyone redoes their presentations and begins to present to each other. You quickly find out what you know and don't know about your client. You also learn that a crucial part of value selling is getting feedback from other sales teams and managers who understand the value selling process. Value selling, more than any sales method, requires the innovation and creativity of others that presenting to your peers can unearth.

In value selling, as long as everyone is on the same page in terms of the process, the focus becomes how well the PSV is developed at a specific time in the deal and for a specific audience. In other words, understanding the degree of PSV development before, during and after the value assessment is very important. Peer group reviews can now be focused on truly helping individual sales teams differentiate themselves in their deals.

Obviously a workshop environment is the best way to learn and experience the dramatic effects of group analysis on value selling cycles.

Other Hard Earned Value Selling Tips

1. Knowing how the value is calculated

    Earlier we talked about how you can destroy credibility of the value if you have too much of it; you run the risk of confusing the prospect and conveying that you are just like every other software vendor out there. Once you focus on the hard dollar value that is specific to the prospects problem, and the solution to that problem, you still need to convey how you came up with the numbers.

In one situation, while working with the prospect's project managers to prepare for a final executive PSV presentation to close the deal, I ran into trouble. I had what I thought was a very focused value statement but as soon as I got into a second level of calculations I lost them. I tried a couple of times more and they were simply not getting it. My value sell, complete with value assessment, seemed to be going up in smoke.

When you hit one of these points the best thing to do is to admit the problem and ask for help. We could do this with the project managers because they were on our side and already sold on the PSV. They just didn't want to get tangled up trying to explain the numbers to someone. They were both people who had to say "yes" when the top executive asks "can you implement it and get the value?".

Once we all calmed down, we suggested that we think about dropping some value points and focus on a few that are likely to be home runs. Then one project manager had a revelation. He remembered a study that the company had done a few years ago, and bought off on, having to do with how much money could be saved in all departments if one duplicate part could be identified and eliminated—about $10,000 per part.

Our PSV had already convinced them that duplication could be cut by about 20% which equated to 2400 parts in the first year. Up to that point we had no idea that the per part savings they were willing to own up to was so large and already agreed to. Immediately we decided to push all other value points to the back and bring this $24 million value point up front.

One lesson here is that you have to work very hard to find prospect initiatives and studies that can contribute to your value sell. The other is that you better be able to present how you came up with the value in a way that everyone can understand. We probably missed the internal study because we didn't do enough work defining the problem.

2. Understanding the power structure dynamics in a value sell

When dealing with C-level value based executives another level of understanding of the power in a prospect organization is required. In one case in a multi-division company, one of the division presidents gave us a "why haven't we done this already" and buy off on a value assessment. Good enough, we thought—this division will buy. We neglected to notice that this multi-division company had a centralized QA function headed up by a person who was in lock step with the CEO of the entire company. This QA VP had to be value sold also and treated like he was the division president's boss. It just gets more complex in the executive suite. You need to do more detective work and background checks to make sure you have the relationships right.

In another situation we started correctly at the C-level and sold the value assessment. The C-level told us to work with the project manager to identify the people who would be involved in the value assessment. Do you remember some advice earlier about this? We missed a crucial step here. We should have worked with the C-level to identify the value assessment players. The project manager appointments were done with a solution sell, not a value sell, in mind and he involved way too many people.

This is where a value assessment can lose steam and become an endless consulting project that is seymour ridden. The resulting endless interview cycles and endless demonstrations usually end in losing the sale or in selling a smaller part of the solution at a discount. The C-level understands this problem because he is value oriented and has experienced endless projects in his company. Once you point out the need for key decision-makers and business process owners you'll get his help. It saves time, generates more bang for the buck, and you keep the C-level actively involved in the deal.

3. How value selling permeates throughout the entire organization

Value selling changes more than just the sales organization processes. Because of the high value and therefore price that solutions can now be sold for, better people can be attracted to your organization. Marketing can support the value sell through a focus on hard dollar value gained by clients. Product development becomes value based because every development project can be judged by it's value to future clients. Value based revenue planning can now be injected into the design of products. One of the best cross-organizational benefits is a focus on value-based thinking and processes that brings the whole organization together with a tremendous increase in productivity.

Chapter 6

Establishing Value Selling in Your Sales Organization

Value based selling will not be able to be established in your organization by trying it out with one sales team, hoping for great results. Just like any good value assessment project, a PSV needs to be put together for the "solution" of value selling. Your CEO must buy off on the PSV for value selling—not just the VP of Sales. The reason is that the CEO will be an active executive sponsor in many of these deals. The CEO has to drive the implementation of value selling through his desire to develop, market, sell, and implement solutions in a value oriented way. Things like a clear definition of the concept, processes, and organization required need to be done before the first value sell is attempted. Value selling, done correctly, can't be tried out—it must be committed to.

Part of this effort is analyzing current sales processes to determine how far you have to go to enable a value sell. Focusing on and analyzing the most successful sales teams that appear to be doing elements of the value sell can help establish a starting point. An analysis of current sales and pre-sales value-based skill levels and the willingness to perform them is required. This process may weed out those who don't want to, or can't, perform the value sell.

A training, mentoring, coaching program is required. I compare this type of change to that of a first time implementer of ERP; they usually don't understand the required education, training, and follow up mentoring and coaching. The organization must commit to the concept of value selling and provide the resources to develop people for it. My value selling workshop can get you started.

Elements of a Training, Mentoring, Coaching Program (TMCP)

The degree of a TMCP depends on the initial assessment of skills and willingness to perform them. You'll find that positioning of and training for solutions will drastically change with a value sell. Some solutions will rise to the top, others will become add-ons, and some will pull other solutions along later, with much higher value for the client. This results in a lot more money being made, with multiple sales and value assessment cycles, with the same clients for years.

Obviously, training on value based selling must be done followed by active observation of those sales teams already accomplished in value selling. This mentoring activity should be led by the salesman and business consultant on the experienced team. "Active" means that after observing presentations and interview sessions the trainees should have an opportunity to perform detailed debriefs with the observed sales team. The trainees should be actively reviewing the days activities and asking questions about all aspects of the value selling that is observed. I always found that travelling with a sales team and debriefing right after the client meetings and over dinner was extremely effective.

The mentoring process builds a lot of rapport across sales teams. That rapport is makes the peer group reviews, that are so essential to value selling, work well.

The mentors and managers perform monitoring and assessment activities according to a schedule of accomplishment. Gradually, performance of significant portions of the value sell will be accomplished and the intensive mentoring activity turns into coaching on an as needed basis.

So, What Did You Learn from This Book?

Hopefully you now know PSV creation and presentation techniques that can be applied to any sales cycle, project, proposal, or promotion. I would also hope that you have a pretty good idea what value selling is and the key concepts behind it. You should have some excellent thoughts about applying value selling to your own deals and to your company.

One of the most important take aways should be insight into the difficulty of value selling. Much higher levels of preparation and teamwork are required. A willingness to be scrutinized by your manager and your manager's manager and your company CEO early in the deal is a necessary evil. This is something many seasoned sales and pre-sales people never get used to.

I trust you enjoyed the surfing analogy. Remember, don't paddle into a big wave—get towed in by your team so you hit the wave at the right point and at the right speed. Don't go out there if there are broken boards on the beach—wait for the right time and conditions—then take the big one home using all your resources, preparation, innovation and diligence.

One final question—did you learn enough to know that you don't want to value sell? If the answer is yes then you have also accomplished something. Value selling requires a lot more guts and ability, not only from a salesperson, but the entire sales team, and the company. The business consultant role has to really step up. The company has to realize that it is probably the toughest role to play in the value sell if not in the company. This is because the business consultant must be a C-level strategist plus a project manager of a value assessment, which can result in detail implementation planning and construction of a statement of work. Do you have business consultants that can do, or have the potential to do, the value sell?

Realizing that you don't want to value sell can actually be a good thing. But before you give up, think about how nice it would be to hear the CEO of a multi-billion dollar company say "wow, why haven't we done this already?" and then not blink when you say "we'll price it according to your value".

The Value of a Value Selling Workshop

My workshop can kick off your value selling efforts. You know the ultimate value: cut sales cycles, work more good deals, increase deal size, and more. At Aspect we were selling software for many times what our competition was getting with a smaller cost of sales, plus the benefit of built-in add on business because of the nature of the value sell. There are up front costs of TMCP programs, building the right teams, hiring better personnel, and the inevitable disruption of a sale or two during the transition. Even with the costs, it becomes obvious that value selling benefits can easily reach into the millions of dollars.

Keep in mind that the workshop is teaching, and allowing attendees to experience, the creation, presentation and critique by their peers, of the PSV approach. As we have said, the PSV approach can be used in many situations because of it's flexibility in emphasizing the "P", "S", or "V" as the client audience requires. So, even if you don't want to value sell, or don't think you do, you can use the workshop to accomplish two things:

1. Qualify whether or not you and your company are a value selling candidate

2. Learn the powerful PSV approach and apply it to your current sales and processes

What follows is a brochure on my value selling services. Show it to your managers and peers to give them an idea of what value selling can do in your company. I've also included a short article titled "Are You Really Value Selling?"; it serves as a good summation of the book and is designed to develop an interest in value selling by telling a story of an early value selling experience. Together they can help you develop an interest in value selling in your company.

Value Selling Brochure

- **Cut sales cycle time,**
- **Work more "good" deals,**
- **Increase deal size....**

**...by selling value
to top executives!**

Value Selling

About *Value Selling*

Are your sales teams prepared for this?

> *"I don't care who you are, who your company is, or*
> *what your solution is—what is the PROVEN value!"*
> -CEO, Anycompany

Value is what top executives want—and the value selling "problem-solution-value" approach creates "hard dollar" solution value:

- Sales teams "engage" with top executives

    - Create a "problem-solution-value" statement causing executives to ask "Why haven't we done this already?"

    - Motivate top executives to manage your sales team's access to the best decision-makers and business process owners

- Top executives hear their people say "Yes!" to "Can you implement it and get the value?"

Value selling workshops show sales teams how to:

- Develop interest through problem determination,
- Develop a solution from the viewpoint of the prospect, and
- Develop value that integrates with the problem and solution.

Your sales teams will learn how to engage with, not merely access, top executives resulting in value selling benefits:

- Cut sales cycle time,
- Work more "good" deals,
- Increase deal size, and...

Price solutions according to their value to the top executive.

About the founder and developer of this approach

Bob Turek is an expert in value selling. As a consultant, manager, leader of sales teams, and mentor, he marketed, sold, and implemented software and consulting solutions priced from $10,000 to $10 million that provide hard dollar value up to $25 million per year.

His published books, articles, white-papers, and hundreds of sales and marketing presentations honed his value selling approach.

Bob's advice helps create the ability to sell solution value to top executives. He has delivered his expertise to enterprise software, marketing consulting, and leadership training companies.

How we work with you

We offer:

- Assessment of your company's value selling potential,
- 1-2 day workshops on how to establish the value selling process in your company, and
- Coaching and consulting to insure that value selling takes hold in your sales teams.

We welcome the opportunity to customize our offerings to fit your specific needs.

We are excited about providing you and your business with value selling skills and tools, that will be used every day, to improve your work and your life.

Value Selling

Contact us

Bob Turek
8128 Clayvale Road,
Agua Dulce, CA 91390

661-268-8808
rturek23@aol.com

Article:

"Are You Really Value Selling?"

Are You Really Value Selling?

By Bob Turek

Value selling!—the latest mantra driven by the tech bust and a slow economy. Smaller prospect budgets demand an excellent and quick ROI. Many times you have to create a budget. So, value selling is all the rage. But what exactly is it? My experience team selling large $5-10 million enterprise software and service solutions revealed that painful changes had to be made by experienced, successful sales and pre-sales people in order to value sell. It is not natural and it involves another level of expertise in planning and preparation that the team was simply not ready for.

Who Cares?

First of all "value" is not on every prospect's mind. And only certain individuals in a prospect company will respond to a value focused selling process. In the process of learning how to value sell we discovered that trying to value sell to what we eventually learned to call "seymours" would basically make them angry. And once you started at that level of the organization it was very hard to move up the ladder.

In one multi-division equipment manufacturer we thought we had a value driven executive. We let him bamboozle us by saying that he was value focused. Actually he was very worried about how his chain of command would assess his "project management" performance, so he wasn't even a classic "feature" guy. Big mistake. Fortunately this company had another division.

We went to that division VP and found him to be a value guy. However, we weren't ready for the value guy mantra, which is:

> "I don't care who you are, who your company is, or what your solution is—what is the PROVEN value?"

Prove it!

After shaking the shocked looks off our faces, we forged ahead with our "same industry" reference who had attained $100 million in hard and soft dollar documented value. Now we expected him to say "wow!" but he laughed at us, and I mean AT us; then he said "prove it!". That call didn't last more than

10 minutes. So, we set up a conference call with our same industry client and the VP and "proved" it.

We waltzed into our next meeting expecting to impress and "trial close" the VP. Then the VP said, "now, prove it in my company". We said, "it will cost you"—and much to our amazement he said "how much?" After that we made our next mistake—we didn't charge enough.

The Value Assessment

A value assessment followed that was basically a large, very cheap, consulting project. It didn't have to be (large and cheap). All we had to do was work with the VP to carefully select a "chosen few" business process owners, who were also decision-makers that he would rely on, to participate in our "project". After plodding along for a few weeks discovering that we were creating a prospect project team quadruple the size we needed, we retrenched and defined the chosen few.

From then on things went smoothly---for awhile. When we tested one of our chosen few to see whether he agreed with our findings, he said that he did and that he could implement it. Then we brought him in front of the VP and he stammered and said he wasn't sure. Thank God for tests. We quickly realized that we had to do a far superior job of "selling" the lower level---we had to do such a good job that when the VP asks the chosen one if he can implement it AND get the value, the chosen one MUST say "yes!" with enthusiasm.

Prepare to Engage

This ability to convince, in a fairly short time, a chosen few that they could implement the solution quickly AND get the value is a key to value selling. Access to a VP and his chosen few is not enough. The team must "engage" with and convince the chosen few by revealing things in a way that they have never seen before. This takes a lot of work in addition to the hard work of asking the right questions and listening to the right answers. It takes a level of preparation that most sales teams have never experienced.

We learned to structure our approach around what we called the "problem-solution-value" statement with the goal of causing executives to ask "why haven't we done this already?". This approach involves a very structured set of activities designed to elicit the key problems to be solved, solution development from the point of view of the prospect, and value development in hard, very hard, dollars. Many mistakes were made; e.g., we put "too much" value up initially confusing the prospect, we talked too much about our solution to the VP who could really care less about it until he had the value, and we failed to initially define the "problem", including barriers to buying, well. All of these mistakes basically caused us to fall down the stairs of the sales cycle a few times and waste untold hours redoing the same presentations. But we finally got it right, and boy, did we learn how to do the value sell.

There were a few turning points. One meeting with a few of the chosen few, who were clearly on our side and helping us determine the value, was going badly. My charts and graphs illustrating the value related to the problem and solution were going way over their heads. Upon seeing this I simply stopped and admitted to my observation. They took a breath, leaned back, and selected one value point. They remembered an internal study done years ago that seemed to relate to it. We took that study, which basically "proved" that several thousand dollars could be saved per part by eliminating "duplicate" parts, and ran with it to produce a "problem-solution-value" statement that resulted in hard dollar value of $25 million per year across all related departments of the company.

The final result took a lot of work; but we learned that if we focus on just a few value items that the prospect is intensely interested in, and prove them out through discussions with the chosen few, we could sell our solutions and services for five to ten times what we thought we could sell them.

And there was the beauty of the value sell—we could price our solutions according to their value to the prospect. In fact, the VP never, and I mean never, asked the price of our solution until he saw the value. This made us understand another truth about the value guys: they could really care less about the details of the solution—they want value.

Value Selling Applies to Big and Small Deals

We later learned that value selling wasn't just for big deals. It can apply to little deals too. It can apply to internal projects. All you have to do is remember to start with a value guy— usually the top or near top executive in the company. Sales cycle time was cut drastically especially where you could "qualify out" early, we were working more "good" deals, and, of course, our deal sizes were zooming.

Here's a summary of the key points made:

1. Find the value guy and impress him or her with a "same industry" value reference

2. Use a "problem-solution-value" approach to "engage" and create value

    Avoid common mistakes:

    > Too many value points,
    > Too much solution detail,
    > Poor problem and barrier definition

    Look for an "internal" study and build a value case with it.

3. Equip the "chosen few" to say "yes" to question "can we implement it and get the value?"

4. Price according to value (but don't tell "seymour" how much it costs!)

About the Author

Bob Turek is a business consultant who works with start up and established companies on strategy, process improvement, and value selling projects. Bob was a columnist for "Intelligent Manufacturing" and has published articles in "The Performance Advantage" magazine. He also wrote *Working the Plan: Closing the Planning and Execution Gap with Rapid Priority Management (RPM),* the first book about RPM, winner of APICS' 2003 Excellence in Innovation Award.

I would appreciate your feedback about the book!

I am very interested in your ideas, comments and questions-please don't hesitate to write to me—Bob Turek at rturek23@aol.com.

123   *Value Selling Business Solutions*